THE ART OF SHOOTING

MAVEN BOOKS

THE ART OF SHOOTING

C. A. Damon

Professional Rifle and Pistol Shot,
Fenton, Mich.

MAVEN BOOKS

Chennai Trichy New Delhi

MAVEN BOOKS

This edition has been published in india by arrangement with Carson Books, UK

ISBN 978-93-90877-54-6

Maven Books
No. 44, Nallathambi Street,
Triplicane, Chennai 600 005

Printed and bound in India

MJP 1014

Publisher's Note

The legacy of a country is in its varied cultural heritage, historical literature, developments in the field of economy and science. The top nations in the world are competing in the field of science, economy and literature. This vast legacy has to be conserved and documented so that it can be bestowed to the future generation. The knowledge of this legacy is slowly gettinsg perished in the present generation due to lack of documentation.

Keeping this in mind, the concern with retrospective acquiring of rare books has been accented recently by the burgeoning reprint industry. Maven Books is gratified to retrieve the rare collections with a view to bring back those books that were landmarks in their time.

In this effort, a series of rare books would be republished under the banner, "Maven Books". The books in the reprint series have been carefully selected for their contemporary usefulness as well as their historical importance within the intellectual. We reconstruct the book with slight enhancements made for better presentation, without affecting the contents of the original edition.

Most of the works selected for republishing covers a huge range of subjects, from history to anthropology. We believe this reprint edition will be a service to the numerous researchers and practitioners active in this fascinating field. We allow readers to experience the wonder of peering into a scholarly work of the highest order and seminal significance.

MAVEN BOOKS

INTRODUCTION.

In writing this book it has been my object to make it interesting and instructive to both the casual reader and the shooting man. Whether you shoot occasionally, or are a shooting "crank," I trust that you will be amply repaid by a careful perusal of these pages. This is not intended as a book of reference for expert shooters, but rather a general instructor to the ordinary shooter and to those who wish to acquire the art. The requirements of this book already exist, and I have tried to write the book to fit these requirements. It must be sufficiently interesting to hold the casual reader, enough in detail to be a practical instructor to the novice, and still not enter into so many minute points as to be distasteful to the fastidious or educated shooter.

I am much indebted to "Shooting and Fishing, of Boston, and its gentlemanly editor, for observations of other shooters as well as the idea of writing a book on this subject. The science of making, loading, holding, and firing, both rifle and pistol, is more fully covered in "Modern American Rifle and Pistol" than is necessary in a work of this nature. Besides it is my intention to handle the subject merely from a professional standpoint, not as a source of income, but as a source of unlimited pleasure and instruction.

One cannot become proficient in any art without there is a natural aptitude in that direction, and a certain amount of pleasure and fascination is derived from encountering unforseen and almost insurmountable obstacles. Then one's pride and ambition are always pushing us forward and are responsible for one's advancement and success. In shooting, as in everything else, one gets along swimmingly to a given point, beyond which all progress seems to be impossible, but after a few weeks or months of careful and intelligent practice, you can look back and see a marked improvement. That is the time when you actually begin to advance, as anyone can acquire what came to you so readily, and what seems to be so easy for a professional shooter, was acquired only through hard work and constant practice. I spoke advisedly when I said "intelligent practice," as it will not benefit you in the least to go out and fire hundreds of shots every day, if you do not study and think of each shot, and if you miss, stop and try to reason out why you missed. Should you hit, it is more necessary still for you to know why you did so, or you will have no idea where to hold to hit again. This applies to all kinds of shooting—Rifle, Pistol and Shotgun, both at stationary and moving objects.

I shall try and put my ideas before you just as if you had never fired a gun and came to me for a course of instruction, the same as you would do to become a musician or to learn some other art where the eye and the hand must be trained to act in unison.

In handling firearms, great care must be exercised to guard against any accident, either to yourself or anyone else, especially your assistant. Always handle any firearm as if it was loaded, and never allow a gun to be pointed towards anyone. Hundreds of people are killed or maimed for life every year by guns that "wasn't loaded." Teach those who are in your company, either male or female, to handle firearms intelligently, thereby insuring themselves and others against accident. Never leave a loaded gun around the house where anyone can come to harm by it. Never have a shotgun with less than four pound trigger pull, as it is sure to be dangerous if handled by anyone unacquainted with it. Then it is liable to jar off on firing the other barrel, if you have both barrels cocked. Never carry a gun cocked while hunting as it is dangerous in the extreme, and if you have a hammerless, keep it "safe;" and practice moving slide or cocking the piece while bringing it to the shoulder.

Do not murder innocent birds or animals merely to gratify your taste for blood, or a cruel desire to take life. There is a plenty of vermin and birds of prey to practice on. Never kill more game than you can use, or kill game while it is sitting. It is more sportsmanlike to kill game while flying or running and it gives the game an equal chance of life, besides showing the superiority of man's ingenuity and skill over the powers of self preservation with which nature has provided all living things.

This chapter can be put into practice without any cash outlay; but if you would go farther, you must make up your mind to part with some money, and the end will not come until you either leave this world of sorrow and woe, or give up your favorite amusement.

GUNPOWDER.

This is an article which has contributed to a greater extent than most people imagine towards the prosperity of this country; it having taken the lead in levelling and cutting for railways, tunnels, canals, aqueducts, parks, and driveways, as well as for the most effective service in large and small cannon, rifles, pistols, bombs, torpedoes, and signal lights by the army and navy; for long distance line throwing by the Life Saving Service, and by fire-works makers for high soaring rockets and special exhibition pieces.

It has been a necessity with frontiersmen and cowboys, and a God-send to an Indian when he captured any. Powder is solely responsible for the disappearance of game, and the appearance of game laws, and occupies a leading position in rifle practice, trap, and live bird shooting, as well as in forest and field sports.

In an early day we depended on England for our powder, but to-day we ship powder all over the world and America stands ahead in its manufacture. Instead of trying to see how cheap it can be made, as in some other lines of manufacture, each mill is trying to excel all others in quality, evenness and a clean burning powder. In black powder Hazard's takes the lead; is clean, strong, and can be had in all grades for pistol, rifle and gun. In nitrous powders, the American Wood is the best; is perfectly safe, clean, gives little report and almost no smoke. I have used it in the theatres and the noise or smell from three drahms was not disagreeable, while Schultz' would drive the people out of the house with the stench and set the scenery on fire at forty feet, and we had to discontinue the use of it on these occasions, and forbid those who competed with us from using it.

SELECTING A SHOTGUN.

In the first place, a shotgun or rifle must be selected to suit your requirements, and no one can pick out a gun to fit you. A friend may advise you and be of great help, but buying a gun is like buying a suit of clothes, in more ways than one. A perfect "fit" is an absolute necessity and can generally be had in "ready made," but can be made to order if preferred. Get as straight a stock as you can use conveniently, as it will give you better satisfaction in the long run and you can shoot it much quicker than a three inch drop, also the recoil will not be as noticeable, although it is there and can only be overcome by light loads or nitrous powder. When you have decided on the price you can afford to pay for a gun, try bringing them up to your shoulder and aiming at some convenient object. Select a gun that you can bring to the shoulder, place the heel plate well in on the collar bone and aim, without stretching your neck or ducking your head. In short, stand and shoot as naturally and gracefully as possible and imitate the desirable features of other shooter's positions. Should it be more natural to shoot left handed, keep it up as it is just as good as any position and will save you time in learning to be right-handed. If you are left handed, your left eye will be the stronger and will help you materially in quick and accurate shooting. Do not nse a nickel plated gun as it will scare the game by the glisten of the sun shining upon it.

The idea of a 10 lb. 10 G, is a thing of the past and is not suitable for anything except wild fowl shooting where very long shots must be made and heavy charges used, and to shoot deer with buckshot when the brush is too thick to use a rifle successfully, and then a 12 G will do just as well. Neither is it advisable to go to the other extreme and get a featherweight as they will soon shake to pieces, unless you pay a good round sum for them. Then the recoil is much more in a light arm.

I got more real pleasure out of a 5½ lb. 20 G than any other gun I ever owned, but would not recommend it for the average shooter on account of the light charge, [2½ dr. and ⅞ oz. shot], which gave a very small killing circle. A 7 or 7½ lb. or 14 or 16 G, or a 7½ to 8 lb. 12 G, will give better results, kill all the game you are likely to get within good shooting distance of. and will be plenty heavy enough to carry all day.

The smaller bore your gun is, the more cartridges you can carry without inconvenience, which is quite an object.

A cheap gun is poor property under any circumstances, and it is not advisable to put a large amount of money into one gun, as it will depreciate in value at least one fourth after the first season's use, no matter how careful you may be of it. Should your high priced gun not suit you for any reason and you wish to sell it, the cash loss would be as much as a good machine made gun would cost. If you bought a cheap gun and wanted to sell it, you will have a hundred chances where you would not have one to sell a high priced one and the depreciation at the same per cent of money invested would be only a trifle. If a man can afford to buy a good gun and pay $200.00 or so for it, I should say get the best by all means, but the forgoing remarks are for the average shooter.

A good machine made American gun can be had from $20.00 up to suit your pocketbook. Get an American made gun by all means, as you can get a better quality and much better shooting arm of home manufacture than can be bought for the same price in imported goods. Then the matter of repairs, if any are ever required, can be easily attended to by mail, while if you have an imported gun, it is a case of calling on a skillful gunsmith who must make the part by hand, at five times the expense of machine made parts. The system of choke boring in use among English makers of low grade guns is not much better than a cylinder bore of American make. You will have to put $150 00 or $200.00 into an English gun to get a perfect weapon and then a $25.00 American machine made gun will shoot just as close and hard as your high priced arm. I know this from experience. You are merely putting the extra money into outside finish and the name of some old English maker. Even if you want a high priced gun, get an American made one, as at the same price home productions can discount European work in design, appearance, balance, fit and shooting qualities. There was a time in the infancy of the firearms industry in America, when English guns were superior to domestic productions, but that time is passed. The oldest and best known American makers are Parker and Lefever. Both are strong, well made arms, hard close shooters, are built to any weight or measure and at any price from the ordinary grade up to $400.00 or over.

Each gun has its special points or advantages over other guns. Each has a style of lock and action of their own and in a hammerless, a good lock is much more essential than in a hammer gun, as the stroke is shorter in the former and if poorly made are sure to cause you trouble. The cocking device, too, is of great importance and should allow the gun to open almost as easy as a hammer gun. In regard to the metal in barrels, I should strongly recommend steel, as it is far less susceptible to rust, pitting or marking, and makes a much tougher barrel than a twist or damascus, will stand more wear inside and out, and more bumps and knocks without denting than will the softer and more handsome looking barrels. A steel barrel if properly choked is there to stay and will not gradually expand where the heaviest strain comes, viz.. at the nozzle, but as it is an elastic metal it will hold its size and not "shoot out," while with any style of a built up barrel of soft non-elastic metal, you will find that, after a few years wear, the barrel has gradually expanded, and the fine shooting qualities are gone, to a certain extent.

Twist and Damascus barrels are merely for the fine outside appearance, but are liable to have minute slivers start up, which were loosened by the boring tool, and did not show when new, which allows rust to get in where you are unable to remove it. Result, a pit or mark in your barrel. With a steel barrel, which by the way, you can pay as much for as you like according to quality, this fault is obviated, as a properly made steel barrel has no grain, being a homogeneous metal without grain, similar to a lead pipe, with equal powers of resistance in all directions, while any built up barrel has as distinctly defined a grain as a pine board, and when any undue strain is brought to bear, it will open with the grain in nearly every instance. Occasionally a barrel will tear along the rib, but that depends on the cause of the accident. Such accidents are generally due to snow or mud in the nozzle, some obstruction in the barrel or coins in the shell when fired. Not once in a thousand times are such things due to any other cause than carelessness, either in taking proper care of the gun, or in loading your ammunition, although the usual crawl out is —— powder.

The sight which comes on all shotguns is of very little ac count and a Lyman ivory sight should be fitted to it at once. This sight is of great advantage as it can be seen in dark cover and after it is quite dark, when a common cross sight would be invisible.

HAMMER OR HAMMERLESS.

The question of hammer or hammerless is purely a matter of taste and price and does not either improve or lessen the actual shooting qualities of the arm. The poorest shooting and most awkward gun I ever owned was an English hammerless. If you are buying a gun for less than $30.00, get a hammer gun by all means, as the expense of making a hammerless lock is much more than a hammer lock, consequently the parts of the gun are slighted in cheap hammerless arms. If you can afford it, buy a good hammerless by all means, if you intend buying a double gun.

REPEATING SHOTGUNS.

If I could have only one shotgun, it would be a repeater, as you then have six shots at your command, almost instantly, and doubles can be made as readily as with a double gun.

My assistant throws six blue rocks in the air, three at a time, all in the air at once, and I break them all with a repeater which is a great deal quicker shooting than it will ever be necessary to shoot at game. When shooting birds it often occurs that a third and fourth shot could be made to great advantage, and with a hammerless ejector it is almost an impossibility. I have seen six single quails killed at a single rise and most of the birds got up at once. Of course everyone cannot expect to acquire the knack of handling a repeater as quick as would be necessary to shoot six shots at a single rise of birds, but with a season's practice, three or four shots should be fired with reasonable accuracy, while the game is within a killing range. Such a gun can be bought inside of $25.00, is practically a hammerless ejector, will outshoot any gun I ever shot at the price, and will out wear any double gun of its cost.

The repeater with lever action is more simple, less liable to get out of order and works much more handy than the slide action, and it can be held to the shoulder and on a line with the game while being worked.

A slide action shotgun cannot be held still while being operated, and if you hold it to your shoulder by the fore stock, as you would a double gun, the action slide will drop back as soon as the trigger is pressed, and a misfire is the result every time. If you do not hold it tight to your shoulder, the recoil will be very unpleasant and the gun will spring up and shoot high. Consequently the only secure hold you have is with your right hand (less trigger finger) on the neck of the stock, and while operating the mechanism by means of the sliding fore end, the muzzle of your gun will describe a circle of from 6 in. to 2 ft. All this is obviated in a lever action. This theory does not necessarily hold good in slide action rifles as the action is shorter and the rifle does not require to be held as firmly to the shoulder as a shotgun, although it is impossible to hold the sights on a small object and work the action of any repeating arms.

With practice, a repeating rifle of 22 calibre can be worked and trigger held and 15 shots fired into an inch bullseye at 30 ft. in 10 seconds. The repeater may not seem quite as symmetrical in appearance or balance when first you try it, but after a few weeks it will seem like a part and parcel of yourself, and can be operated without a thought. Until you can work your gun, sight, and shoot without stopping to think, you will never become a good wing shot either with shotgun or rifle. I am so accustomed to judge quickly in shooting, that I find myself estimating the proper distance to hold ahead of every bird that flies past me within shooting distance. By constant practice one becomes accustomed to estimate distances, speed of flight, etc. of game without a thought.

Many of my remarks, such as choke boring, drop, trajectory, etc., may not be clearly understood by some of my readers who are not accustomed to handling firearms, but lack of space forbids my going into detail and teaching you the A B C of shooting and also have you graduate in the art of shooting, all in this little book. Many of my readers will be better informed on these subjects than I am, and to stop and explain each technical expression in detail would become a bore to the experienced reader and my object would not be attained.

CARE OF GUNS.

When you have bought a gun it depends entirely with yourself whether it will last and keep its fine appearance and shooting qualities or not. Any well made gun will last a man a lifetime if properly cared for, but once neglect it and the trouble will commence which can never be overcome.

Neglect to clean a gun properly, leave a little flake of lead or burned powder in it, forget to look at it occasionally, or worse than all, lend it to your particular friend, and it is on the road to ruin. Nothing but a thorough cleaning and oiling will keep a barrel bright on the inside. If you use water in cleaning your gun, use it boiling hot. If your shotgun is loaded, use a brass wire brush, or better, "acqua ammonia," on a rag, on your wiping rod. Rub until clean and dry and oil with sperm, vaseline, or Winchester gun grease. While in the field, if your gun or rifle becomes caked with burned powder, give it a bath, internally, and go on with your shooting. A little water run through a barrel loosens all dirt and the first shot removes it and will do no harm.

A rifle requires much more work to keep clean than a shotgun, and the smaller the bore of the rifle, the more bother you will have with it. In cleaning, always use a damp patch first. Clean thoroughly, oil and set in a dry, warm, place, and always keep a gun in a cloth [or sheepskin, with wool on inside] case. Sole leather bags and boxes are good, if you can afford them.

Never plug the barrels up as the metal is sure to sweat, and if there is no escape, moisture will form and rusting commence. Keep emery out of your guns under all circumstances. It takes an expert gunsmith to use it properly.

After your gun has been set away two or three days, get it out and clean with dry rags and oil again. Repeat this operation twice and your gun will not take any harm in a year, but don't neglect to look at it occasionally. Fine cleaning tools will make your work easy, but elbow grease is the main thing. Some people advocate leaving a gun dirty from shooting, and cleaning only when you are ready to use it again. This is a wrong idea and should never be tried. Burned powder, if kept dry and perfectly air tight will not rust a piece of metal; but such conditions are impossible in a gun barrel. The action of the atmosphere and moisture contained therein soon cause burned powder to undergo a chemical change, the result of which is an acid and very destructive to iron or steel.

Aluminum in gun barrels is very much an experiment at present, but it has several advantages over steel. It is much lighter and more rigid than soft steel and is not effected by the powder which ruins so many of our barrels now. Steel, copper, and aluminum coated balls are an experiment, and their use is to keep a ball from flying to pieces or stripping in rifles of small calibres, such as the .301 and other military rifles when large charges of smokeless powder are used and a high nozzle velocity of 2,000 feet a second and upward is obtained from a barrel with a 12, 10, or even an 8 inch twist.

In cleaning a revolver, the cylinder should always be removed and the notches for cylinder stop should be kept free of grease and dirt, as the accuracy of the arm depends to a great extent on the proper working of the cylinder stop.

Never tinker or experiment with a firearm because it does not suit you. There are plenty of guns and if it does not suit you, dispose of it and get another, as life is too short, and where experiments are being tried, too uncertain, to try and improve either the gun or the ammunition.

Reloading and Cleaning Tools.

In buying your reloading and cleaning outfit, do not be taken in by the nickel plated finish of the tools, or the oily tongue of the salesman, but choose such tools as it is necessary to have, of the best, as they will be the cheapest in the end.

A priming tool for paper shells should have a post to slide the shell over as the head is not strong enough to stand the ring tool generally sold.

For brass shells, the cheap tool will answer.

The Ideal loading flask is the best thing for measuring powder, as it will give you an accurate and uniform load from five grains to 5 drahms, besides shaking the charge down into the smallest possible space. The same company also make a full line of reloading tools, resizing dies, and special sizes and forms of bullet moulds. Their dipper is an absolute necessity to make perfect balls, and their "Hand Book," which they mail free, gives many "pointers," which all shooters should know.

In running bullets, the same temper should be obtained that the factory use. This can be ascertained by referring to the factory catalogue, and the proper amount of block tin should be added to your load and the metal must be as hot as possible without being red, and the moulds also must be perfectly free of oil or any other substance and hot enough to "blue."

Nothing but practice and experience in reloading and shooting, can make you successful in reloading your own rifle and pistol cartridges.

For lubricant, use that which the Winchester Co. sell, or make it from tallow, parafine and beeswax, of proper hardness to suit the season, but do not have it too soft at any time of the year.

Each gun company makes reloading tools for their own arms, but if you wish an adjustable tool or special mould it can be had of the Ideal Co.

In lubricating bullets, a lubricating pump will save lots of work and cramped fingers, besides doing the work much better than can be done by hand.

Where shells are to be used a great many times and with light loads, it is advisable to fill the cavity around the primer pocket with solder. This must be done before the shells have been used or immediately after being thoroughly cleaned.

Put a drop of tinner's acid and a small piece of solder into each shell and set them on a hot stove until the solder flows and fills the crease. Do not put too much solder in, or it will fill the primer cavity and have to be cut out. This makes a shell almost everlasting, saves buying new ones, is not much trouble and makes a sure fire.

To clean brass shells, use ammonia one part and rain water three parts, but never use acids, as they kill a shell in a very short time. After cleaning, rinse thoroughly in hot water and put in a warm place to dry; an oven is best. The primers should be removed before the cleaning process.

When shells become swelled or bent, do not file or hammer but use a resizing die. Clean the shells and press home in the die with a vice and do not drive the shell in with a hammer.

The original package of cartridges tells you what size of primers to use, and by pulling a ball, you can see what grain of powder to use in reloading. Fine powder will make a shotgun scatter, because it burns too fast and gives too high initial velocity. The same thing will happen in a rifle using a large charge. For light loads of 8 or 10 grains in .32 to .44 revolvers or rifles, the finest grain powder should be used. For loads up to 30 grains, use F. F. G., and for all larger sizes of cartridges use F. G. powder.

Never use a nitrous shotgun powder in a rifle as good results cannot be obtained. Nitrous powders are perfectly safe, if used according to directions; but if you try experiments with it or overload, it is at your own peril.

A slight increase of charge in black powder merely gives a little more recoil and report while an increased load of nitrous powder is liable to become unruly.

In loading shells, do not try to force too much powder in, and seat the ball home, as the powder is crushed and packed so tight that good shooting is an impossibility. Then you are liable to swell the shells so they will not enter the chambers of your rifle, and cause trouble.

For short range shooting when light report is desirable, light loads and round balls will give good results in most any rifle or revolver.

If the shell is straight, seat the ball on powder, and if a taper shell, seat ball in mouth of shell and lubricate, leaving the 8 or 10 grain charge loose in the shell. The great drawback to such loads is the excessive fowling.

For loading Colts, Martin and Winchester model 90 repeaters, the "Lightning Loading Tube" is of great advantage, especially when one is in a hurry or in a gallery when one's time is valuable. These tubes are of brass throughout, well made, and every one tested. With this tube a repeater can be loaded with 15 cartridges in three seconds. The 15 cartridges can be loaded into the magazine just as quick and easy as one can be put in by hand.

This tool can be appreciated by anyone who uses a .22 repeater, as it is only 12 in. long and can be carried full, in the pocket. There is no spring or rod to get out of order as the tool is very simple. This tube is fully protected and can only be had of the author, as it is not handled by the gun dealers.

RELOADING SHOTGUN SHELLS.

No one can tell you how to load your gun to get the best possible results, as there is just as marked an individuality among guns, even of the same make, as there is among men of the same nationality.

You will often see an article in shooting papers in which the writer advocates some particular powder, wad, shell or style of loading, as the only one on the market worth using.

He has simply found out the most favorable conditions for securing the best possible results for one individual gun and thinks it will give the same results in any gun. It may suit your gun and it may not. Try it and see if it is any improvement.

In reloading shells in damp weather be careful and dry the shells on the inside as they will be moist and that will deteriorate your powder and on unloading a misfire you will find the shell full of paste instead of powder.

Never try any experiments in shooting buckshot, shot concentrators, solid balls or wire cartridges in a choke bored gun, but use a good safe load of loose shot crimped well down so that the shot will not rattle. The men who made your gun and ammunition knew a great deal more about the business than you do or ever will, as they have expended many thousands of dollars in experiments and when you buy a good grade of goods you get the benefit.

Get good powder and do not be saving of your wadding. I would rather sacrifice both powder and shot than scrimp the wadding.

Three drachms and one ounce is a good load for a 12 gauge gun, and one drachm and $\frac{1}{4}$ more shot is sufficient for a 10 g.

I once owned a $5\frac{1}{2}$ lb. 20 g. and it was a splendid shooting gun with 2 dr. and $\frac{3}{4}$ oz. No. 8 shot, but would not shoot any other size satisfactorily.

A gun may shoot one size of shot extremely close and even and not be of use with other sizes, but if it shoots 6 S. well, it will generally shoot all even numbers of shot well. The same applies to odd sizes.

After seating your primers well down, put in a uniform load of powder and a cardboard wad on top of it. Seat this wad well down with rammer and mallet, if you are using black powder, but if using any nitrous powder, follow instructions on the package, and use double strength primers. Now put down a $\frac{3}{8}$ in. felt or two common black edge wads and another cardboard on top, and press firmly so that no space is between any of the wads. Not that space is dangerous, but you will need it for your shot and crimp, and if any was left, the wadding might allow the shot to rattle after your work was done.

See that your wadding is even and level or else your charge of shot will go out on the same angle and scatter.

By having a solid cardboard each side of your elastic felt wadding, you get the impetus of the powder explosion behind the wadding and the resistance of the shot ahead of it, which causes the wads to expand and form a gas tight joint so that all the energy of the explosion is utilized.

On top of your shot load, place a regular shot wad if it is to be had, as it goes to pieces immediately on leaving the muzzle of the gun.

If this wad is not to be had, split a felt wad and put the cut side next the shot and crimp tight so that the shot cannot rattle. The load may be varied for different shooting, and when a satisfactory load is found, stick to it.

For short range shooting, when a large killing circle is required, the best results are obtained by overloading with shot and using a heavy wad on top of shot.

Lubricant is just as necessary on the edges of these wads as it is on a bullet, and for the same purpose, viz., to lessen friction, leave a smooth, oily surface for succeeding charges to pass over and to prevent leading and excessive fowling.

TRAP SHOOTING.

Trap shooting is a pleasant and manly amusement and is the best manner to acquire the knack of quick and effective handling of a gun. While a man may become a fine trap shot and may be a very ordinary game shot, or vice vera, it is very extraordinary to see a man who is an expert at both kinds of shooting.

A man generally prefers one kind of shooting and that is what he will excel in, and as it is a matter of pastime and amusement only, it is advisable to stick to the one which yields the most pleasure.

From a financial standpoint, trap shooting is like horse racing in more ways than one, and the best shots do not always come out a winner.

THE RIFLE.

The rifle, and its numerous attachments, represent man's highest mechanical achievements. It has taken a more prominent part in opening up new countries, destroying dangerous animals, subduing hostile men, both civilized and uncivilized, and in providing food and amusement than any other weapon. It is sensitive to the slightest defect or carelessness in holding, sighting, judgment or loading.

The possibilities of a fine rifle is something wonderful and the amount of pleasure to be derived from a true rifle cannot be estimated.

The long range rifle I am not able to discuss, as I have never shot over 200 yards and only a limited number of shots at that distance.

In writing this book it has been my intention to write of my own experience and observation, and not to resort to other people's experience or theories.

No one man can become equally proficient in all branches of rifle, pistol and shotgun shooting, and a man who is a good all-round shot and can hold his own in all branches with the average shooter in each of the different clubs, is a phenominal shot. Such a man I have never yet seen, and probably never will.

One becomes accustomed to the weight, hang, pull, sights, recoil and trajectory of a rifle, besides going through the motions of reloading without a thought, and on taking up a new rifle he has it all to learn over again.

By constant shooting and a large variety of guns to use, one may become broken in so that he can shoot with most any gun, but will have his favorites for different kinds of work.

We will allow you to pick out the action of a rifle which pleases you best and fits you.

The most popular rifles are the Winchester, Colts and Marlin, which are made in all sizes from 22 to 50 calibre and suitable for all kinds of shooting.

Do not get too long a stock on a repeater as you cannot work the lever without taking the gun from your shoulder.

A single shot costs less and will cost you less for ammunition, as you will take more pains with each shot than if you had fourteen more ready to be pumped out. A single shot is less liable to break down, as there are fewer pieces, and more shots can be fired in five minutes with a single shot than with a repeater. Also 50 shots can be fired quicker and more accurate with a single shot than with a repeater.

Several things are required in a cartridge; accuracy, flat trajectory and killing power, and if one only of these points is required the others must be sacrificed.

A.

Accuracy requires a heavy ball, weighing about 5 times as much as the powder charge, as the following target cartridges will show: 32 cal., 40 gr. powder, 185 gr. ball. 38—55—255. 40—50—265. 40—70—330. 44—105—520.

These are all paper patched balls and for target shooting only, and the barrel must be wiped after each shot.

B.

Flat trajectory requires a very light ball and the high speed attained gives it the name of Express.

Also a hollow pointed bullet is an express and may have an explosive primer put in the ball if desired.

The hollow pointed ball goes to pieces on striking a bone, and the explosive ball acts like a miniature bombshell inside of dangerous game.

Such a rifle has a very flat trajectory up to one hundred and fifty yards, but beyond two hundred yards the accuracy is gone and the drop of bullet is very fast.

When a ball of this class had become perfectly useless the ball in class A. would be flying steadily on its course.

A 40—110—260, or a 45—125—300 express, have less than 10 inches trajectory at 200 yards and the smashing powers are somothing terrible.

The 38—55—255 has a 14 inch curve, and the 45—70—405 has just a foot at the same distance and much more accuracy.

Here we have the two extremes, high curve and accuracy at long ranges, even up to 1000 yards, and flat, rapid flight to 200 yards and useless beyond that range.

The first are good only for target shooting at known distances and the latter for game shooting where no time can be taken to adjust sights, and a shot is seldom fired at over 150 yards.

C.

I have given you the two extremes, which are the height of perfection for what they are intended, and now will give a list of cartridges which are more likely to meet the requirements of the average shooter: 25–20–77. 32–40–165, 38–56–255, 40–65–260, 40–82–260, 45–75–350.

These rifles are accurate enough for hunting, will keep ten shots on an eight inch spot at 200 yards, have good penetration and the recoil is not excessive.

Never think of buying a rifle larger than .22 that shoots a rim fire cartridge, as the expense of ammunition will more than overbalance the saving in price of the arm.

If you want a nice little rifle to shoot squirrel and for snap shooting, get a .22, if for hunting small game and should you want to kill a lame horse or occasionally a bull, the .25 will do the work, if you are a marksman, if not, a .32–40 will be more effective.

If you are going into a deer country do not stop short of the .40–82 or 45–75, and you will not miss it with either of them.

An express is not worth a cent in brush shooting, as a twig no larger than a straw will send your bullet wild, but it is the proper thing in an open country. Many northern and wertern hunters use an S. S. of large calibre and carry three shells between the fingers of the left hand and can fire four shots with accuracy nearly as quick as with a repeater.

When shooting, great care should be taken to avoid sending balls singing in all directions, as a ball cannot be accounted for after striking any obstruction or even water. It never continues on its original course, and is liable to do damage in any populated country.

The ideal combination, all round rifle and shotgun suitable to shoot anything from a humming bird to a grizzly, has never yet been made and never will be. Such guns exist only in the addled brain of some sporting paper correspondent.

If you have a variety of shooting, you must have a variety of guns. If you cannot afford the guns, then you must get one which nearest fills the bill for all your requirements and get along with it.

For such a rifle, the .25 is at the head, and in a shotgun a 14 or 12 g. of light weight will do good service.

One combination which has been a great source of pleasure to me is a good gun and a bicycle.

The rifle case can be strapped on the wheel so as not to rattle and be out of the way and can be easily withdrawn.

With a wheel you can hunt over more country and do it easier than in any other way.

Another essential thing for every shooting man to do is to subscribe for a good shooting paper.

I don't mean a "sporting" paper that you would be ashamed to allow your wife or sister to read, but a Sportsman's paper, which they will look forward to with just as keen an interest as yourself.

They may not read all the adds as you will; but will thoroughly enjoy it.

For a rifle shooter, Shooting and Fishing, of Boston, will give you the most useful information. But if you are interested in dogs etc., try the American Field, of Chicago.

COMBINATION GUNS.

The only practical combination gun is the double gun, one barrel shotgun and one rifle; as the three barrel gun is sure to be set wrong and requires too much manipulation.

The double rifle is not practical, as one which shoots its two balls parallel is very rare and I never happened to see one. Even if it was perfect, a repeater is better, as when the double gun is empty it is useless, and a repeater will shoot fifteen times as rapid as the double gun will two.

I once saw a repeating 12 g. rifle being made by the Winchester Company for a British officer in India for elephant and tiger shooting, and it was as fine a weapon as any one could require for such a purpose. It was built on their shotgun frame, and used paper shells with 6 dr. of powder and an ounce explosive ball.

Pocket Rifles.

Pocket rifles are long barreled pistols with a skeleton stock which may be readily detached.

Excellent scores have been made at two hundred yards with .22 long rifle and .25 cartridges in a 12 or 18 inch barrel.

It makes a handy arm to carry in a satchel or can be readily carried in the pocket.

Pocket rifles come under the head of pistols as some are used as both rifle and pistol by merely putting on or taking off the stock.

With an 18 in. barrel using the .25 cartridge, five shots have been put in a four inch ring and ten shots in an eight inch ring at 200 yards, shot at a rest.

This is good shooting, even for a rifle in the hands of an ordinary marksman.

No sportsman's outfit is complete without a pocket rifle.

Revolver and Pistol.

The revolver is an American invention and thus far we have succeeded in keeping the championship with this weapon among our own countrymen.

It is very valuable as a weapon of self-defense and in times of war as a weapon of offense.

Revolver and pistol shooting is a distinct branch of the art and requires more practice and experience to become even an ordinary shot than to become proficient in any other branch.

It is the highest possible attainment to be able to do good all around pistol work at short and long range target work and at game and snap shooting.

Target and game shooting with a pistol are as much different as trap or game shooting with a shotgun.

As a pastime and amusement for ladies and gentlemen, pistol shooting is bound to hold a place which nothing else can fill.

Your lady friends will enjoy the sport as well as yourself if you have a good weapon and take pains in showing them how to aim and pull the trigger and if you are not careful to keep in practice, they will outshoot you in a week's time.

A lady who once makes up her mind to learn to shoot, and takes pleasure in it, will become a good shot in less time than any man, if she has a painstaking, intelligent instructor.

In teaching one to aim a rifle or pistol, there is nothing as good as a rough pencil sketch showing front and rear sight and bull's-eye above so that top of front sight is just even with notch in rear sight and aiming at six o'clock on the target.

The term of time of day in target shooting applies as if you were aiming at a clock dial. Twelve is top, three is right hand, six at the bottom, nine to the left, etc.

The first thing to consider is what calibre and weight of an arm you want, and that is to be governed by the expense of ammunition, facilities to shoot at short or long range and whether the recoil is liable to overbalance the pleasure to be derived, and whether the noise is liable to become a nuisance to others or disagreeable to yourself.

The .22 short will do good work at ten to twelve yards, but the long rifle cartridge, or Winchester Rifle will outshoot it at any distance and cost more.

A .25 R. F. cartridge is a very fine one for fifty yard work, is clean, has a low trajectory and enormous penetration for so small a size, but is very expensive.

Next comes the .32 and .38 S. and W, cartridge and the full grown .44 S. & W., Russian model which is recognized the world over as a military and target cartridge.

The last three have straight shells and admit of a light load if desired. This gives you quite a variety of shooting with only one arm.

The .44 meets my requirements and gives me better satisfaction than any other size, as it is easier to keep clean, can be used with 8 grains of powder and a 120 gr. round or conical ball. This does not recoil in the least and is accurate up to 10 yds. but beyond that, the trajectory is too much for accuracy and more powder must be used.

A 10 gr. load with same ball will do excellent work at 20 yds. and also kill small game.

Then if you wish to do 50 yard work you have a weapon capable of making the possible, viz. 6 shots in a 3 in. ring, although you may not be able to hold it so as to secure a bullseye, in a dozen shots when you commence.

Notwithstanding the great number of so called "revolvers" made in this country, there are but two recognized makes of first class weapons.—the Smith & Wesson and the Colts. The former is preferred by many amateurs and experts on account of its ease of manipulation and more symetrical appearance, and for some time it was the only make that had target sights fittted to it at the factory, and it has held the world's championship for years as a target revolver.

The colt has a solid frame and will stand more hard knocks and abuse than its cousin, the S. & W., consequently, it is preferred by the western people, cowboys, etc.

Again, the Colts is susceptible of that kind of shooting known as "fanning" which is holding the trigger and striking the hammer with the hand, while the S. & W. cannot be cocked while tbe trigger is held back. An expert can fire six shots from a single action revolver in less time than it is possible to shoot a double action revolver the same number of shots.

These different features have their advantages and disadvantages in both arms ; but for the work for which they were designed, both are as near perfect as it is possible to make a revolver.

The Colts have a .38 and .41 with solid frame and the cylinder swings out on a crane and can be emptied and reloaded almost instantly.

I had the pleasure of shooting No. 1 of this pattern, which was a hand made revolver for a pattern and it was a superb shooting and working weapon.

In shooting a revolver, aim as with a rifle, at 6 o'clock. Do not grip the handle too tightly as it will make you tremble, but always hold with the same pressure. Press the trigger gently until it is nearly to the firing pressure, as you are moving your sights up the target, and at the right instant apply the pressure required to fire the arm, but do not jerk the trigger as it will throw you off.

After shooting a month or two do not get discouraged because you cannot equal the scores published in the shooting papers, as they are either the work of professionals or amateurs who devote themselves exclusively to this branch of shooting, or a scratch score which could not be duplicated in a life time.

Another class of phenominal scores are pure and simple lies. I know of one man whose scores and targets have appeared from time to time in sportsmen's papers, purporting to have been made at a regulation distance and target, when I know that the man is not capable of any such work, as I have seen him shoot his best,

Such people generally get brought up in the long run and I have had the pleasure of calling several of them down and shall continue to do so whenever the opportunity offers.

The above does not apply alone to pistol shooting but to all branches. Like all other sports, shooting is indulged in by all classes in this free country, and a small percentage of the "sporting-man" element has crept in ; but if a man wants to know the meaning of "hospitality and courtesy," let him be a good shot and go into any town or village in America, be gentlemanly and decent and look up the right party or club, make himself known and show his ability, and he will be treated as well as it is possible to treat a fellow being.

There is a good fellowship among shooting men that does not exist among any other class, be they either rich or poor.

The remarks on revolver shooting cover the ground on pistol shooting except as to the different makes, as revolver makers do not make pistols, with one exception.

SIGHTS.

In rifle shooting the sights are a very important feature and those furnished on the rifle as it comes from the factory are generally very crude affairs. The quickest sight to catch is a perfectly flat bar with a half round notch. This can be made by filing the original sight down flat and reducing the breadth also.

For a front sight the Lyman hunting sight is the best thing. If you want a peep sight, Lyman's again comes to the front with the best thing on the market ; but always use the large aperture as it is much clearer and just as accurate as the smaller one.

The flat bar and ivory bead are best for pistol and revolver shooting.

For shooting at any distance with peep sight, a wind guage is desirable and Lyman is simply perfection as you can have the large aperture with light ring around, or the wheel as on any peep sight.

A rifle should be sighted so that by holding a fine sight at the bottom edge of bullseye at your shortest range shooting (20 yds. for .22, and 50 yds. with hunting rifles) the ball will hit the center of the bullseye, then you will not have to elevate your sights for double the distance, but merely hold "dead on" at anything up to double the distance you are sighted at.

Beyond this distance you must know the trajectory of your rifle, and if the distance is not known, you must estimate as nearly as possible and adjust your sights accordingly.

Set your rear sight in the center of barrel and bring your rifle to shoot into line by driving the front sight.

If your rifle shoots to the right drive your front sight to the right. If to the left, reverse the operation. Should your rifle shoot too high when a very fine sight is seen, the back sight must be lowered, and if too low, file off top of front sight.

Great care must be used in driving the sights, as your barrel may be ruined by carelessly driving a sight.

When a sight has been filed or has worn bright remove it, polish bright, pack in a tin box filled with leather scraps, put the cover on the box and burn in the stove until it quits smoking, then take off the fire and drop into a bucket of water. This will put on a dark blue and a very thin case harden.

When your rifle is sighted perfectly, take a very fine cold chisel and mark the sights and barrel so that the slightest variation can be noticed and corrected without the trouble of shooting and driving sights.

If you prefer an open sight, get one which is flat on top with a half round notch.

The V shaped notch is an abomination, as are the buck horn rear sights which are of no benefit and only obstruct the vision.

Manufacturers make what the greatest demand calls for, and as the present demand is for a CHEAP arm, they must meet it, and in doing so something must be sacrificed.

For their own interests, the shooting qualities are kept as good as possible and the remaining parts are made with an eye to strength and cheapness, consequently the awkward stocks and poor balance of cheap guns. But if you will put sufficient money into any make of arms you will find them poems of grace and symetry.

Unless you have shot with a telescope sight, you never have realized what rifle shooting is. There is a great amount of pleasure in watching a woodchuck or squirrel wink, at 50 or 100 yds. and know that by pressing the trigger you can kill as sure as if he were within 20 ft. of you.

When one learns to understand the trajectory of his rifle

and estimate distances it is very little trouble to shoot small game at 200 yds. with a telescope sight, as the glass helps you to find the game, aim at it and spot your shots so you know whether another shot is necessary or not.

For general shooting at all kinds of small game and vermin a .25-20 with telescope is the height of perfection.

The Moggs telescope is the best as it is made of a solid drawn steel tube and not liable to get out of order or get bent.

SHOOTING CLOTHES.

If you have not a partly worn grey business suit to use as a shooting suit, a dead grass colored corduroy shooting suit will give you the best service at a reasonable price.

They should not fit tightly anywhere and especially at the arm holes. Have large solid pockets as they are much more convenient than a cartridge belt and will carry your ammunition with more ease than having all the weight on the hips.

For upland shooting, a good pair of shooting shoes well hob nailed, lacing at instep and on the side, will be comfortable and will keep you dry in slush or snow.

For ducking or woodcock shooting, a light hip rubber is the thing. Wear a soft hat of the same material as suit and never get a double ended helmet as it is no protection to your face and runs the rain down your neck. Because a man is out shooting it is not necessary for him to be dressed like a tramp, and look so that he is ashamed to go to a farmer's house to dinner.

If a man exercises common sense and behaves as a gentleman should, he will never get turned off from a farm, except the occasional crank which you are bound to meet in all walks of life, and with a little tact, even he can be managed.

SNAP SHOOTING.

Snap shooting is hitting objects on the move, with a SOLID BALL, either from a rifle or pistol.

Shooting with shot cartridges is not snap shooting, but deceiving the people.

All horseback shooting at balls, etc., tossed in the air is done with shot, as no man living can hit often enough with a ball to make an interesting exhibition.

The American people want to be humbugged and they are not satisfied without they think someone is being nearly killed for their amusement. Consequently we have the holding and head shots and the cigar shot, as we must please the people, to draw our salary.

Although many of my shots look very dangerous, I guard against all accidents and use all the precautions possible, look carefully to guns and amunition, use a helmet for the head shots etc., reducing actual danger to a minimum.

The first thing necessary for snap shooting is a .22 repeating rifle and one with the "left hand" or fore end action is preferable as you can work it with more speed in double and treble shots, etc.

A Raub trap and 500 card board targets which are good for 10,000 shots is the next thing.

To begin with, the targets should be thrown 10 or 12 ft. high and the shooter stand about 15 ft. away and try to shoot 3 or 4 inches under the target, after it has started down.

No one can hit the target with any regularity, as it is turning, as the space of time is too short and in throwing the rifle up, you will throw it above and shoot too high.

Throw the rifle up as soon as the target goes up, and follow it until the target is nearly ready to stop. Stop the rifle about one foot below where you think the target will turn and directly in its path coming down and shoot when it is 2 or 3 inches above your sights.

Do not try to get a fine sight but see both the sights plainly and practice bringing the rifle to your face until the sights will always come in line and in the same place.

The farther an object drops, the faster it travels, consequently after a target has fallen 10 or 15 ft., you must hold from 5 to 6 ft. below it according to the weight of the object and the velocity at which your ball is flying.

With a .22, you must hold nearly twice as far under as with a .44 and in shooting two or three times at a tin while in the air, different calculations must be made for each shot and that at almost lightning speed.

Nothing but constant and careful practice will make a good snap shot of you and until the rifle can be operated and fired at objects in the air without a thought, or being conscious of pulling the trigger, you will never become an expert.

A steel ball is made for this work which rings when hit, but is very dangerous, as the bullets glance from it and your assistant is liable to get a "spatter" of lead.

I might write out every motion and explain every shot, but it would be of no help to you, as each person must learn these things for himself.

Coin shooting is the hardest of any snap shooting, as the object is small and the holder hardly ever gets two alike in one show, to toss up. Consequently they are tossed uneven and on the curve. In coin shooting I use a .44 repeater, as it punches a hole through a coin when a .22 would only dent it.

Another object in using a .44 is that it makes more report and attracts more attention.

A .44 will generally knock a quarter out of sight, as the coin is so light it will fold around the ball and go ahead of it rather than be punctured, while a half dollar will only fly a few yards and fall to the ground with a piece cut out, if hit on the edge. or a hole through it if hit near the center.

By the curve, I mean that the coin or target does not travel up and down on a perpendicular line, which calls for another quick calculation on the part of the shooter to get directly under it.

Some people shoot while moving the rifle and others hold it nearly still while firing the shot. I prefer the latter style.

In firing three or four shots at one target, one shot must be fired on the way up, one at the top and the others as you can catch them.

I have seen a quart tin hit four times at one toss.

A very quick shot is to drive a ball or block out of the water with one shot and hit it with the next while in the air, but a large calibre rifle must be used.

All kinds of contortions, positions etc. in exhibition shooting are put in to suit the shooter's taste and with a little practice are just as easy as shooting from the shoulder.

Shcoting from the hip is all in practice and judgment, and one can acquire wonderful proficiency in a short time.

Shooting with a card over the muzzle is very simple and is done by shooting with both eyes open and the card seems to disappear.

Always shoot every kind of fire arms with both eyes open as by closing one eye the range of vision is obstructed and the eye which you are sighting with is sure to squint.

As an example of what can be acquired by practice I will cite one of my shots.

I use a 12 ga. Winchester repeating shotgun at 40 ft. from a Raub trap and have broken 8 out of 10 targets blindfolded. This seems quite strong to the ordinary shooter ; but when the theory is explained it is quite simple.

The targets all fly in a straight line and turn within six inches of the same place.

I get the bearings from a cleat nailed to the stage, which points directly towards the trap.

My constant practice enables me to throw my gun up to the proper height and by counting 1-2-3-4, from "click" of the trap I get the cue for firing.

Such shots, although very difficult are not appreciated by the average audience as they think there is some "fake" in it, and they want a man to break every target thrown in the air, regardless of its size, or the wind which may be blowing a gale if one is showing out doors.

The "Wild West" costume and big hat which most shooters wear, do not make them cowboys, by any means ; but is merely worn to attract attention and please the audience, as a man cannot give as good satisfaction doing a shooting act in a dress suit, as in a sporting costume.

I do not know of a professional rifle or pistol shooter who is a cowboy or western man.

Because a man comes from the west, he is generally supposed to be a fine shot ; but I never saw a western man who was a real fine shot with a revolver or a snap shot with a rifle.

Some time ago an article appeared in "Shooting and Fishing" of Boston, on the "The Proper and Absurd Use of the Rifle." and the author claimed that all exhibition and snap shooting should be abolished, etc.

I claim that entertaining an audience with the rifle and pistol is just as legitimate a calling and use for those weapons as entertaining an audience with a violin, or on a trapeze, as comparatively few people can acquire sufficient skill in any one direction to be able to entertain an intelligent and enlightened audience, and when one possesses such skill, it should be cultivated to the highest possible degree.

www.ingramcontent.com/pod-product-compliance
Lightning Source LLC
LaVergne TN
LVHW010435230826
846092LV00009BA/1169

* 9 7 8 9 3 9 0 8 7 7 5 6 0 *